The Unseen Realities

Angels

An Unseen Reality

Rich. N. Ekegbo

Ploughman Publishers Awka.

Angels an Unseen Reality

First Published, January 2008

ISBN: 978-978-48450-0-7

Ploughman Publishers,
76 Arthur Eze Ave (Opp. Emma Nnaemeka Junction), Awka.
Phone: 08082406727,
Website: www.igboniile.org
E-mail: richploughman@yahoo.com
P.O. Box 62, Amawbia, Awka South L.G.A,
Anambra State.
Nigeria.

Specially Dedicated to our unseen guardians, the *Holy Angels,* and *their devotees*.

&

Mr. Paschal Chiegboka for sponsoring the publication of this book.

TABLE OF CONTENTS

INTRODUCTION

INTRODUCING THE UNSEEN REALITY
It might be odious to picture a chasm without a link, a river without a bridge, a storey building without a staircase, or even Jacob's heaven without a ladder (Gen. 28:12). Such concepts could assume the picture of the great gulf between the good and the bad in the world of Abraham, Lazarus and the Richman in their yonder world (Lk.16 :26).

But on the other hand, God has bridged the gap between us and Himself, and between heaven and earth with the angelic beings, the existence of which this little book tries to prove within the limits of its scope, or rather within the scope of its limits. And now, not only Jacob's world is linked to heaven with the aid of the ladder and the angels, but the entire world down to the present.

The first part of this book therefore, tries to look into and through the history of some religions that believe in **Angels, the unseen Reality,** and how they use that doctrine to shape their entire belief system. Through this enquiry also, we will be able to see some subtle similarities in especially the religions in question. In this reading, the knowledge of **Yin_Ayan** is very important in understanding not only the classes of the bad and the good angels, but also the ups and downs of life with its attendant good and evil (people) respectively.

5

The second part of this book centers on **Angels, An Unseen Reality,** generally in Christianity, and in the Catholic Church in particular. And the church which with humility, does not claim originality to the belief, however, cites references to the bible, draws inferences there from and moulds the doctrine on angels, which she dogmatizes in her faith as found in the Catechism book. The final chapter of this section gives us some examples of how the holy angels, under God's command, protect us even beyond our earthly pilgrimage.

The final part of this book tables some ecclesiastically approved prayers that help us to extricate ourselves from the grips of the wicked angels and spirits, and draws us to God through the media ship of the holy angels. In this case, I acknowledge the adoption and adaptation of some ecclesiastically approved prayers to the angels from some sources in this part also.

Have the protection of the angels. Amen.

Fr. Rich.

PART ONE

I.   **THE UNSEEN REALITIES**

II.   **ANGELS AS SPIRITUAL BEINGS**

     ANGELS; *A MYSTERY IN HISTORY*

"Look, I bring you news of great joy, a joy to be shared by the whole people." Lk. 2:10

Angels An Unseen Reality

CHAPTER ONE
THE UNSEEN REALITIES

*Only faith can guarantee the blessings that we hope for,
or prove the existence of realities that are unseen.*
                                                    -Heb. 11:1

The greatest problem facing the average believer, not just in Christianity, is the difficulty of believing what he should doubt, and sometimes, doubting what he should not doubt to believe; or to put it better, how to believe what he is not sure of its existence. The Catholic Church had already arrested this problem by the promulgation of her doctrines and dogmas. Nevertheless, even within the ambience of the Catholic Dogma, and outside the prescriptions of the other non-Catholic faiths, in heres the idea of the unseen realities, asking for more attention.

The realities as laid down by the author of the **Letter to the Hebrews,** in extension, include aquatic realities, terrestrial realities, atmospheric realities, and at the level beyond the visible, the celestial realities. These

9

realities which are often translate as "powers" and which are often seen as "unseen', that is the "unseen powers", make the human body and soul their field of operations

Thus, sometimes realities are the forces of goodness or harmfulness unto man.

The unseen realities, which include electric current, wind, cold, radio, heat, waves, spirits, phantoms even angels and other unseen forces shape our lives for better or for worse. Sometimes these forces may not be something, though; all the same, they should not be seen as nothing.

Seers, mystics, believers, scientists and even philosophers often cipher, decipher and or discern these forces, including their modus vivendi and modus operandi. Although they may be more than discernible, faith, vision, knowledge and to some extent, sense experience testify to seers premonition of activities of the evil one, activity of the angels of God, mystics interaction with elemental spirits via their astral travels. And even philosophers, exemplified in Leibniz and his belief in his monads, try to convince us of the influences of the unseen realities. The scientists in their own world, which you call laboratory, have succeeded in mystifying, and to some extent, deifying some "concepts" like atoms, protons, neutrons, electrons, unicellular "realities" like bacteria, fungi, amoeba, and the like, as powers which radically change things for good or for bad for man. The two convictions they need from us are that we can hardly see or know much about these concepts, unless we are "insiders"; and that these concepts are the bases of the changes we see in the visible world.

The Hebrew writer needs only our belief in unseen realities. Moreover, when we have seen, we not only believe in their activities within *our system,* but also have to go beyond that.

Even the providing powers of radio, television, and telecommunication services, suggest to us that there are some linking forces somehow, albeit invisible. There are possible contact points between man and man in such ways as shaking of hands, hugging, exchanging blows, wrestling, mothers breast feeding or lapping their children and so on. On the other hand, the unseen beings which angels and demons

11

are part of, do something or fail to do something to us in similar ways. Various religions, including some of those of non-literate cultures, have beliefs in intermediary beings between the sacred and the profane.

In Pagan religions, spiritual beings are often seen as benevolent or malevolent according to the circumstance of a person, group of persons or even races. Thus, when one is affected as such, one often inclines to sacrifices; either to appease or thank the being in question.

However, it is in the religious world that we have to be most careful because of the sensitive nature of the belief in the unseen realities. Yes, this is because the issue at stake deals not only on matters that concern only the body, and to some extent the psyche as we have already seen; but rather, the unseen realities that are involved in religion has to do with the soul, good and evil, angels and demons, God and Satan goaling towards either salvation or damnation.

THE CONCEPT OF YIN_YANG

The Chinese tried to stress the unholy marriage between the force of evil and the force of goodness in their concept of **yin**

_yang, stressing the difficulty of arriving at pure goodness in nature. Yin_ayan is always represented by a semi-circle of two colours, each overlapping the other.

In Eastern thought, **Yin_yang** are the two complementary forces, or principles, that made up all aspects and phenomena of life. **Yin** is in even numbers as the valleys, and seen as female; and is represented by tiger, the colour orange, and a broken line. **Yang** is in odd numbers, as in mountains and seen as male; and it is represented by the dragon, the colour azure and an unbroken line. The two are said to proceed from Supreme Ultimate (Tai Chi); their interplay on one another, (as one increases the other decreases vise versa), being a description of the actual process of the universe and all that are in it. In harmony, they are depicted as the light and dark halves of a simple circle. The concept **Yin_Yang** is associated in Chinese thought with the idea of the five agents, or elements (Wu hsing): metal, wood, water, fire and earth. The concept of these ideas lends substance to the characteristically Chinese belief in a cyclical theory of nature and human events.

From the third century, the significance of **Yin_Yang**, has permeated every aspect of Chinese thought, influencing astrology, religion, divination, medicine, art, and government.

Etymologically, the word Angel is derived from the Greek word άγγέλος, meaning angel, or messenger, the idea of which was borrowed from the Hebrew word, לת ד (mal'āk), meaning the same, angel, or messenger.

The idea of Angelic reality which was very early developed in Zoroastrian religion, influenced Jewish religion which in turn influenced both Christian and Muslim religion with the same respect.

The concept of angels, though slightly different from religion to religion, is still of much universal importance, especially to these mentioned religions. In all the religions, however, the good angels play similar roles of ministering to God, guiding the people on earth, and acting as go between in man's relationship with God. With similar understanding, these religions view as benevolent the spiritual beings of power or principles that mediate between the realm of

14

the sacred, the transcendent realm and the profane realm of time, space, causes and effects.

Zoroastrianism was founded by Zarathushtra (Zoroaster), about the year 1000 B. C. Zoroastrianism, has another names as Mazda (Wise), the name of the religion's Supreme god, or Ahura Mazda (Wise Lord). This religion originated in the Eastern and South-Central regions of the Iranian world, between the great mountain ranges of the Hindukush, and Seitan, and is today divided between the Iran and Afghanistan. Therefore it was the religion of the Iranians under the rule of the Iranian-speaking Aryan populations, member of the Aryan, or Indo-Iranian group of the more extended Indo-European family.

In Zoroastrianism, there was a belief in the amesha spantas, or the holy or bounteous immortals, which were functional aspects or entities of ahura mazda, the wise Lord. One of the Amesha spantas, Vohu Manah (Good Mind), revealed to the Iranian prophet, Zoroaster (6th Century B. C.), the true God, his nature, and a kind of ethical covenant, which man may accept and obey or reject and disobey. In 17th century Europe, various

15

demons were listed according to their powers to entice men to what were called their basic instincts or desires. Included in such lists were nightmare demons, demons formed from the semen of copulation, and demons who deceived persons into believing that they could perform transactions (nocturnal flights to sites of sabbats, alleged rites of witchcrafts). The alleged demons noted by the prevailing religions of the world are the gods or spiritual beings that succumb to, or were overpowered by the dominant doctrinal views of a conquering people. Thus, the teutonic, Slavic, Celtic, or Roman gods that were reduced to demonic antagonists of Christ, his saints, or his angels were absorbed by the cults of Christian saint figures. In Eastern religions, such beings include avatars in Hindu religion, and the bodhisattvas in Buddhism.

The development of the notion of angels in Judaism owe much to Zoroastrianism both in form and content.

> Judaism adopted the Zoroastrian division of the universe into three realms; heaven, earth and hell. Heaven is the celestial region inhabited by God and his angels; earth, the terrestrial world of man, limited

16

by time, space, cause and effect; hell,
the subterranean world of chaos, darkness
and death, the abode of Satan and His
demon followers.[1]

The good angels that are living with God in heaven have greater knowledge than men. They serve and praise God always, reveal the divine truth, extend the divine will to man, reward the good, punish the wicked, and conduct the souls of the righteous into heaven.

Jewish religion also holds that hell is the abode of the fallen angel Lucifer and his cohorts. These fallen angels were once faithful to God and ministered to Him until they revolted and were consequently rejected and ejected out of heaven

And now war broke out in heaven, when Michael with his angels attacked the dragon. The dragon fought back with his angels, but they were defeated and driven out of heaven. The great dragon, the primevial serpent, known as the devil or Satan, who led all the world astray, was hurled down to the earth and his angels were hurled down with him. **Rev.12:7-9**. And thus, they go all out tempting sons and daughters of men (cf. ! Pet. 5:8).

17

The Old Testament, which is also a version of the Jewish religion, is familiar with such expressions as "hosts of heaven" and "The Company of divine beings." In the apocalyptic literature of Judaism that describes God's dramatic intervention in history, seven angels; sometimes-called archangels, lead the heavenly hosts. These seven, noted in the non-canonical First Book of Enoch (chapter 20) are Uriel (leader of the heavenly army and guardian of sheol, the underworld) and Raphael (guardian of human spirits). Others are Raquel (avenger of God against the world of lights); Michael (guardian of Israel), Sariel (avenger of the spirits); (Gabriel ruler of paradise); the seraphim, (and the Cherubim); and the Ramuel also called Jeremiel (guardian of the souls in sheol). Of these, two (Michael and Gabriel), are mentioned in OT. Raphael and Uriel were mentioned in the Apocrypha, a collection of non-canonical books.

From the Jewish tradition of angels, Christianity developed its own tradition, so that apart from Jewish idea of angels, archangels, seraphim, and Cherubim, five other spiritual powers were added according to the letters of St. Paul. And these powers are thrones, dominions, principalities, powers, authorities, all of which the Christian Theology together refer to as the Choirs of angel or the Hierarchy of angels. As objects of devotion, special attention is paid to Archangels Michael, Gabriel, and Raphael in the Roman Catholic and Eastern Orthodox churches.

Islam also developed the hierarchy of Angels in the defrayed order of importance. The four throne bearers of Allah (hamalat at arsh), is symbolized by a man, a bull and an eagle and a lion in Islamic legend (which draws from Images of John's revelation in Apocalypse). The other two include Cherubim (karubiyun), who praise Allah and four archangels, Jibril (or Gabriel, the revealer); Mikal (or Michael, the provider); Izra'il (the angel of death); and Israfil (the angel of the last judgement); and lesser angels, such as hafazah, or guardian angels. Islam classifies spiritual beings into angels (Malai'kah), demons (Shaytaatin), and djinni, or genies. The last group are the spiritual beings that might be either benevolent or malevolent. By cunning, a superior use of the intellect, or magic, a man might be able to manipulate a djinni for his own benefit.

In African Traditional Religion, angels are regarded as God's messengers. These messengers of God have peculiar roles to perform. The Africans who have the wide spectrum of angels, have different ideas of their names and likeness in accordance with the region and culture of the different parts of the continent. Generally the names and roles of the angels accrue to them in accordance with the actual significance which they represent, projected, universally by the universality of phenomena for which they are being revered, such as earth, sky, thunder, land, sun, water and so on. Thus, they are believed to wield a great influence in the issues within the ambience of their jurisdiction.

> ...the divinities are ministers, each with his own definite portfolio in the Deity's monarchical government. Each in his own sphere as an administrative head of a department. They are also intermediaries between Deity and man, especially with reference to their particular functions.[2]

CHAPTER TWO
ANGELS AS SPIRITUAL BEINGS

*Another day, the sons of God came
to attend on Yahweh and Satan came
with them too. - Job 2:1*

Reality is the word, which explains that something is real; that is that something can be seen, felt, and usable to the extent that even the blind or the dumb can be convinced of its existence. Within the class of things that are real, there are things that can be proved with sense experience, while others must depend on higher sense of imagination, which is faith in action, to reach the level of accepting the fact that they exist. The former lies within the power of the senses and of philosophical enquiry that is understanding in order to believe; while the later, which is to believe in order to understand, depends on the power of faith. Most of the contents of this category are the existing unseen realities.

We should not be skeptical to the extent of disbelieving everything we cannot see. Blessed are those who do not see, yet believe, not only the risen Lord, but unseen realities. Descartes doubted everything except doubt itself. The Church defines faith as the supernatural gift of God, which enables us to believe without doubting whatever God has revealed. Nevertheless, it is possible to doubt that God reveals everything. Someone who doubts that God reveals everything can possibly believe that the devil reveals too. Yes, I mean that it is possible to believe that it is God that reveals the contents of revelation and other contents of our faith. But it is possible too, to doubt God as the source of the revelation of the pranks played by the monkey in your maize farm, the apparent truth from the hide and seek played by kids, the answers to the cipher, and even the conditional demands of the devil in return for something to be done. In **Psalm 13**, the foolish fool did not take the time to look up, before he concluded that there is no God above. God may after all be there, and it is also possible that he could not see Him, especially if he has serious problem in his belief system.

Revelations and realities continue to remain independent of whether we believe them or not, and whether we accept them as such or not. The real issue or issues is that there

22

would be wholeness, only when there is at least, a passive interplay among what is believed, the reason for believing, and the believer; otherwise a reality and what it is, and what it does, continues to remain there for only those who have something to do with every particular reality. Now, it is not too easy to remove doubt from Thomas, for he must not have been too sure of the Lord and His resurrection and the attendant Good News, so he had no need of staying back and wasting his precious little time with other disciples. The fact is that as the I AM is, what are will continue to be, independent of whether we accept them or not. But the problem is that our not accepting, sometimes, what we have to accept, makes the forces through which the realities operate take us by storm; and so those who are not ready jump at the sudden blow on the door or even at the ringing of the telephone. The advice of John Daly, the presenter of the Real TV tallies with this, "you do not know when the reality might happen."

As a philosopher, I was made to understand zero better. When it was being philosophized about, it was said that zero is not nothing, though it is not something. Moreover, as good as it later came to be seen, I later came to know that the figure "0" is not something if it comes before any other numeric figure, but it is something if it comes after any figure that is not zero. Therefore, zero is not nothing and it is not something anyway. You cannot find, say a zero penny, lying on your path, as you can find one that the woman in Jesus' story found when she swept her house. Even in your composition, you can interpret the figure "O" as anything. And even when it is represented in its synonym, naught, or its full name zero, it might not suggest something serious; yet what makes but little meaning when it is written, say 001, is perfect by a hundred percent when it is written as 100. And so, inasmuch as we cannot discuss with, or even see the unseen realities, we need not doubt that they exist; for the proof might still be found in common sense and faith.

The unseen realities can be as numerous as the tangible objects that are seen. Therefore, to doubt their existence as good as doubting the existence of the visible trees, sand, water, and so on. What I am talking about is not outside the plane of the visible realities, rather with faith, beyond man and his environment, lies the invisible realities, angels and demons in their own, or rather in our own environment.

It does seem that since the creation of the world and the definition of God, as the unmoved mover, everything has continued to move, to act and to change in the air, on land, even in the Heraclitus water where everything has always been in perpetual flux. Everything, even if not in discernible constant change, at least, in perceivable constant activity. The words of the Modern Philosopher, Henry Bergeron, stipulate that to be alive is to be active, which invariably means that to be active is to be alive. As such, the activities of supernatural realities are always felt even when they are not observed. The reference above gives us the reason to believe that every spiritual pure reality has some form of activity to perform, and some mandates to fulfill for better for worse for us. Where we mortals in this fallen world get it all wrong, is when and where we think and believe that all the immortals must plan and play, or rather play and plan for the good of man. Long as we live in this sinful world, we must always try to bear in mind the antithesis there are in light and darkness, truth and falsity, hardness and smoothness, white and black, saints and sinners, ups and downs, good and evil, and of course, God and Satan. Nor should we be so saintly to think that Satan, who came along with the children of God, came to be assigned to preach repentance and salvation for the children of God. No, rather, we should know that the constant activities of angels and demons should serve as a further boost for us to step up our faith and activities in faith's direction.

When asked who is the owner of this world, God or Satan, the catechumen answered, both God and his servants, even the evil ones. Even the creation account tells us the story of God and goodness as well as Satan and evil. Nevertheless, the notion of who owns the world should not be contested better than one can contest in the law court, his shirt which his servant is laying claim on.

Perhaps by faith we have God as one and the only Father and creator; but by consideration, the same God considers giving at least fair treatment to each and everyone of his children. Satan is not a saint, nor will he ever be. Job knew that, but perhaps he did not know that the fiend had a hand on his ordeal. Yet the ignorance of that did not make him not to fight to a good finish the battle of his life and that of his faith. Like Job, each man should brace up for the battle against all the forces that means

26

to face him. St. Paul in his Epistle to the Ephesians reminds us that, we are battling against the principalities and the ruling forces who are masters of darkness in this world, the spirits of evil in the heavens. **(cf. Eph. 6:12)**. Faith has provided us with the awareness of the presence of our fiend, therefore, our hope in what is laid in store for us in future, should equip us with the courage to wrestle in the present, to finish like Job.

The Angelic Reality

The monotheistic religions of Zoroastrianism, Judaism, Christianity and Islam conceive a tripartite universe of celestial, terrestrial and subterranean. This view has influenced Western man's concepts of Angel as well as his scientific and metaphysical concepts.

In the Biblical, Hellenistic world, (that is Greco-Roman culture), and Islamic understanding, the terrestrial realm was a world in which man was only given small chance by time, space, power, ability, and causes and effects. Planets mostly occupy the celestial realm, which is made up of seven heavens or spheres, the living area of God and spiritual beings. The subterranean, or where is commonly known as *under the earth* is believed to be the area of confusion and the resting place of the spiritual powers of darkness. At the highest area of the heavenly places is regarded as the highest point of the sacred or holiness. That is the dwelling place of Yahweh, the God of Judaism, whose name was so holy that it should not even be spoken; Bythos, the unknowable beginning beyond beginnings of Gnosticism; the heavenly Father of Christianity who is known through his Logos (the divine Word or reason, Jesus Christ); and Allah, the all powerful, the Almighty and the sublime God of Islam.

The message of these religions is usually on what is revealed. That is the highest being, and on the destiny of man according to His response. Because of their understanding of revelation or otherwise, angels might attempt to deceive man with false revelation as we see in Eden when the Devil Deceived the first man and woman **(Genesis 3:5)**. Or on a good note, reveal the truth about man's true nature (identity), origin and destiny, as we see in Angel Gabriel when he brought the good news of God's plan for man to the Blessed Virgin Mary. **(Lk. 1:31-32).**

28

The monotheistic religions we are talking about, regard the angels that present to people the wrong aspect of the message from God as malevolent in function. Such malevolent angels are what Christianity calls the devil, and what Islam calls Iblis; this devil or Iblis took the form of a serpent in the Biblical story of Eden. Later interpretation of this story explains that the devil's aim was to make man not to know his abilities or limitations as man.

What tempts to put some bit of complacence in the attitude of some believers of the unseen reality is the psychoanalytic adventure into the understanding of the unseen reality. Thus this modern understanding tempts to psychologically explain away the unseen realities, including the angels.

Recently, many Christian Theologians are using these forms of analysis to explain the primitive and traditional belief in angels and demons. In the light of this type of interpretation too, they explain the tripartite cosmos of celestial, terrestrial and subterranean structure as forms of mythology. This mythological explanation operates in tripartite structure of human functionality. And when broken down, the tripartite structure gives rise to three aspects of man which are

29

the ego, (the conscious aspect of man), the superego (the restrictive social regulations that enable man to live as a social being), and the id or libido (a seething, boiling cauldron of desire that seeks to erupt from beneath the threshold of the conscious). According to this re-interpretation, demons can be seen as the projections of the unregulated drives of man that force him to act only according to his own selfish desires, taking no account of their effects on other persons. In other words, if a person does not control himself, he would just tend to be selfish without considering the rights of others. For the average person, demons can be defined as the environmental and hereditary forces that cause man to act, think, and speak in ways that are contrary to the wellbeing of himself and his community.

In his book, **The Devil's Share**, the modern French writer, Denis de Rougemont, explained that the devil and the demonic forces that plague the modern world can be well documented as modern man's return to barbarism and man's inhumanity to man. In the 2nd century A. D., Clement of Alexandria, who was a Christian Philosophical Theologian, said that demonic forces often captivated man by the inner appetitive drives of his passions and bodily desires. The Freudian "myth of the human personality" and other psychological studies have thus initiated another way of studying angels and demons.

Medieval iconography, which showed angels and demons in drawings, the way that they were very clear to all who saw them, had been replaced by psychological, psychoanalytical, and modern mythological symbolism coupled with Theological reflection.

As religious beings we believe that there are unseen realities which we commonly refer to as angels and demons which we may not too wrongly take to be the initiators of goodness and evil respectively, which is translated into **Yin_Ayan,** the Chinese version of evil and good in the world.

In the physical world, man and animals represent the physical realities, which we can view as living things. Even insects have their own natural inclination to goodness and badness. In the level of man, which is the king of the seen realities, and who on good note, is made in the image and likeness of God, we have good men and evil men; and often we do not wait for Angel Gabriel to tell us more about them. The forces of goodness dwell inside of

31

man but only show itself in his actions; so that a man can either be said to be good, gentle, virtuous, truthful, loving, or bad, callous, deceitful, mischievous, and evil. In Zoroastrianism, the Persian religion, frogs are the bringer of plagues and the Ahriman, the power of darkness, in his struggle against the Ormuzd, the power of the light.

Nevertheless, in the order of the pure beings, the created spirits, we have the good and the bad spirits typified in the angels. Even within the class of angels, we have the good and the bad angels. And within these two, man can convincingly know that both physical and spiritual war rages on about him of which often times, man is helpless. About this, we should bear in mind that the dynamic factors in healthy spirituality are love, wisdom, courage, and prudence. Not surprisingly, these are also the elements in the dynamics of goodness. These factors intimately interlink with healthy identity and integration; a crucial fact often overlooked unfortunately. The opposite elements involve unhealthy religiosity as well as the dynamics of evil.

The Evil spirits and Demon Spirits

The forces of darkness are often referred to with common names as demons and evil forces, or even the devil. In some places they are referred to with proper names.

Demon is from the Greek word, Daemon, which means a "supernatural being" or "spirit". Though it has commonly been associated with an evil or malevolent spirit, the term originally meant a spiritual being that influenced a person's character. An agathos daemon ("good spirit"), for example, was benevolent in its relationship with men. Socrates spoke of his daemon as a spirit that inspired him to seek and speak the truth.

However, The Old Testament has such common name as Belial. This name means unworthiness and was personified as the leader of forces of evil and the adversary of God. Demon spirit appears as Satan in the Qumran before the notion was adopted by St. Paul. Insinuating what it does, St. Paul was tempted to ask, "How can Christ come to an agreement with Belial and what sharing can there be between a believer and an unbeliever?" **(11 Cor. 6:15).** The Bible also records other names of the evil spirits as, "son

33

of the morning, the anointed cherub that covereth, Satan, Lucifer, Devil, Enemy, Adversary, Serpent, Oppressor, Deceiver, Liar, Beelzebub, ruler of Demons, the God of this age, the son of perdition, the accuser of the brethren, and Brlial." [3]

It is interesting to note also that the Vulgate uses the name Abaddon to refer to Satan as the "destroyer", while the Septuagint, using the word, Appolyon, describes the same concept as "the angel of the bottomless pit."

Perhaps there is no other book of the Bible, in both Old and New Testament, where there is more interplay of the forces of good and bad than in the Book of Tobit. In this paticular book, the Demon with the particular name, Asmodeus has been wielding its power over the people of God to such a degree that the intervention of the Archangel Raphael was very much needed to ward off the fiend. Before the intervention of God to save the family of Tobit, and other good parties, including Sarah's family therewith, have had their woes in turns, *For she had been given on marriage seven times, and Asmodeus the worst of demons, had killed her bridegrooms one after another*

34

before ever they had slept with her as man and wife. **(Tob. 3:8)**

Generally the force of evil in whatever guise or names it assumes, in whatever age or ages it operated or operates, only inclines to distort the serenity of nature and do harm to the human soul. That is why St. Peter warns the Christians to beware of the devil and all its antics **(cf. 1 Peter 5:8).**

> In Greek, one of the commonest titles of Satan is Ponēros, *the evil one*, the one who deliberately attacks and aims to destroy the goodness of men. [4]

Different cultures and religions look at the power of the evil one as varied as its modes of operation, so that any contact, not only with the evil one itself, but any object that comes in contact with him, is already bewitched. Hence the essence of many rites and rituals in many religions, at least to ward off his advancement in any form. This means that in a bid to preserve culture and religion and keep them to the least defiling status, every race tries to be wary of any form of contamination arising from any contact with the evil one. This means that caution and precaution are always spelt out to people. And when by any act of commission or omission, a person or group of persons commits what would serve as a loophole through which the devil would sneak in, there is always the call for appeasement with sacrifices.

The Jews see the wilderness as where the devil has his resting place on earth, ...*the mention of the desert reflects the belief that wilderness was the habitat of evil spirits.* [5]

So wilderness is identified as unclean, so that it wouldn't surprise us to know that lepers are driven to the wilderness and the dead are buried there. When the men had driven the scapegoat to the desert, during sin offering, they were required to have bath before they rejoin the worshipping community.
(cf. Lev. 16:22).

Like the Jews some other cultures, like the Igbo before the advent of Christianity, drive those who have developed tumor, those who beget twins and some people who suffer from some form of mysterious sickness to the wilderness. In most cases too, the Muslims bury their dead in the wilderness, just like some other believers.

36

What makes the understanding of the spirits or demons more difficult to man is man's inability to be sure, whether spirits have organs like humans and whether they appear like them. Man would have been contented to assume that they operate in mediums, as those who claim to see them and know them, try to make us believe during their rituals. *We must distinguish between evil angels and evil spirits. Angels have spiritual bodies. Evil spirits have no bodies - in fact they try to enter bodies.* [6]

All are not angels that are spirit, but all angels are spirit in nature. Before we get down to guardian angels, we must note that there are other beings that assume the shape of angels. These include the spirit beings; some of which have different appearances. In the apocalyptic book of revelation, there is countless number of these beings, some are good, but some are bad in their activities. The good angels, no doubt, have their rewards, just as the bad ones have their pay. We must be very careful not to regard all the destroying angels, such as those who slay the first born of Egyptians, as bad angels, rather, we should note that they are but carrying out instructions. But on the other hand, the rebellious angels, tend to bring destruction into any place that has godly order.

37

However, they will still be compensated for their rebellion.

The prophet, Ezekiel, noted that the "Cherub" that "covereth" became a rebel, a being of violence and sin, God brought him to Ashes upon the earth." **Ez. 28: 11-19.** In the book of **Genesis 6:2,** the sons of God which were typical angels of God, admired the beautiful ladies on our earthly plain, from where they were able to peep out. The beauty endowed to those ladies misled those bloodless and fleshless beings. They were consequently rejected and ejected from their natural status to come to live with men on earth. The end to that episode became the marriages between angels and men; and the last result is the production of the Sons of Anak, which are people of extraordinary size and stature **(Num. 13:33).**

The mention of such beings as Cherub, Seraphim, Archangels, especially in the apocalyptic and prophetic books will convince us to know that there should be more to such beyond the scriptures in the Old Testament and in the New Testament. And lessons like these suggest to us that angels are created and so prone to evil even in our age of contemporary Christianity. But however and whenever the extraterrestrial beings act, much still holds in reserve to the faith of those who come in contact with them.

THE FORCES OF GOOD AND EVIL

From celestial, down to the subterranean, there is no doubt that some massive interplay of forces, contained in what can better be seen as a world where the celestial, atmospheric, terrestrial and subterranean worlds and their forces are wound together. In this interplay of the even and odd forces, good and evil, visible and non-visible, holy and profane, light and darkness are in constant friction and sometimes in constant disharmony.

The book of Genesis, after recording the creation account stated that, "everything God created were good." That's not withstanding, the world goes on to feel the effects of the activities of the agents of darkness. Apart from the Bible, which seems to be near successful in locating the coming of evil at Eden with the fall of man, many schools of thought in history have made many fruitless attempts to get at the origin of evil in the world. St. Augustine as an individual and as a serious investigator, could not trace its origin, and with frustration at the end of his fruitless search, pleaded with his audience to accept man's limitations in certain things, especially with regard to that.

From every day experience, every man encounters what he sometimes deem good and sometimes what he sees as wrong and evil. The problem is more on the fact that apart from things that proceed form God's goodness, whom Aristotle calls the unmoved mover, there are many things within this all encompassing world, which move to move others, so that it is always difficult to know what moves what leads to evil, in both visible and in invisible worlds. In a local epic lyric, we used to argue about what happens to the tortoise (Nwaliga), which also included why and when they happened. To bring to the fore, the idea of causes and effects, we say that the breadfruit seed fell on the tortoise Nwaliga. And to bring the poem to its best, we sing that the blacksmith made the gun, and the gun killed the kite, the kite carried the chick and the chick ate the termite, the termite ate the walking stick, the walking stick broke the breadfruit, and the breadfruit fell on the tortoise Nwaliga. Of course the end result of Nwaliga is death. Inasmuch as we are not concerned about the importance, economic or otherwise, of the elements in the question about tortoise Nwaliga, the supremacy and the role of each of the elements in question is brought out somehow and terminates in the effect, giving a rough idea of causes and effects of the unseen realities in our own physical world. But within the context we are discussing, we discover that often man does not know some causes; and often too, he feels the effects of some causes, perhaps due to his limitation of knowledge.

The physical gospel of Tsunami, constant earthquakes, landslides, erosion, storms, hurricane and similar forms of mishaps, which we call natural disaster, are what man often with serious probing could proffer but little believable reasons for. The people that receive the effects suffer some defects or die as effect. Sometimes we hear about **UFO,** (Unidentified Flying Objects), which was recently explained away as nonexistent phenomena; even when some good books in your nearest good library had furnished you with something about it. It is not to be seen with the simple logic of what is or what is not since the knowledge is yet to be cleared as it was in the case of Copernicus and the sun. yet, such sensational experiences and phenomena, which occasionally take place in various points of the world begs at least a little attention from us the tangible creatures.

41

Sometime in 1977, in the area of Carajas mining project, there used to appear blinking lights in the wee hours before dawn. These lights blinded and drained the blood of the landless peasants, (in that state of Maranhao), to whom alone they appeared. Because they could not know anything about this phenomenon, the locals called it chupa-chupa, which however is only a reference to the creature's addiction to guzzling hemoglobin. In his book, **The Order of the Day,** Marcio Souza recorded the spread of the Chupa-chupa. *in 1978, it appeared in Vigia and in Mosqueiro, in the neighbouring state of Para. And in order to have the privilege of a close encounter, all that was required was any sort of proof of membership among the disinherited of the Earth. By the following year, it had already spread to Amazon State, with sightings in Paritins and later in Maues. At the moment of this writing, it has become bold enough to occasionally startle farmlands from Iranduba, a municipality just outside of Manaus. And the Capital itself has not been immune to nocturnal visits: wandering lights have been robbing the sleep of slum dwellers from Coroado [sic] and Compensa to Gloria and Sao Jose.* [7]

42

On 8th day of March 2007, in Neni, an Anambra town in Nigeria, a fallen tree which refused to be sawed, revolted against the operator and the sawing machine that was to have been used against it. It was reported that after the revolution and after the cobra that appeared from the trunk had pursued away the eye witnesses, the tree which fell down a year before stood back at its former base. Although unlike Thomas, we are not bound to see forces in operation with our poor human eyes, but since we always feel their effects, we are bound to accept that they exist in good and bad forms.

We are daily being faced with some hard facts, which we cannot just wave away with the simple wave of the hand, even though we cannot give explanation or proffer solutions to them. We should note that neither the midnight free call of the **MTN**, nor the pay as you go by the day, does furnish us with further information about the route through which the telephone message travels. The only thing we know about the journey of the message that reaches us, is the little tangible electronic idiot in your hand, which we call a telephone handset. Now the television system and the radio system are as good as the telephone system; and their messages are convincing enough that what they present might be a copy of something, which is of course something you had only known something about.

PART TWO

I.   ANGELS IN THE CHURCH

II. THE HOLY ANGELS ARE OUR BEST FRIENDS

III THE GUARDIANSHIP OF THE HOLY ANGELS

ANGELS: *A MYSTERY OF FAITH*

"I am sending an angel to precede you, to guard you as you go and bring you to the place that I have prepared." Ex. 23:20

CHAPTER THREE
ANGELS IN THE CHURCH

The existence of the spiritual, non-corporeal beings that Sacred Scripture usually calls "angels" is a truth of faith. The witness of Scripture is as clear as the unanimity of Tradition.- CCC 328

Anyhow, it might be a little problem to have faith only to some extent about certain realities. And so, it becomes a big problem to know whether to have full faith or partial faith in some realities. When I was in a minor seminary, and before I took my West African School Certificate Examination, I was taught that iodine is a solid element that can only be seen and touched in its solid state, but that when the element is made to re-act with the application of fire, it automatically melts, sublimates and disappears as smoke as in Abel's sacrifice. I was also convinced that this too was how metylated spirit and even phenolphthalein volatilizes from their liquid to gaseous state when they are exposed to atmospheric condition, which could even be as low as twenty-five degree centigrade. Angels too, are spirit, only that they are not metylated. But, they can appear and disappear according to the allowed situations. That is why it seems very difficult to be convinced about their existence, just as it is difficult to be convinced of the existence of the will-o-the-wisp; or to convince the blind to believe in the existence of mirage, which we seem to see but cannot grasp.

We are not only concerned about how we believe in angels or otherwise, but what the mother Church has not said against them, and or what she has said about them so far.

The church has not told us to disregard any spiritual being or revelation as such, but rather to be cautious in referring to them. The first letter of St. John warns us thus, *My dear friends, not every spirit is to be trusted, but test the spirits to see whether they are from God.* **1 Jn. 4:1.** We should also know that God has not advised us to adore angels; and angels themselves know that. In fact angels deprecate any worship that people wanted to direct to them. The Roman curia gives and explains the proper approach due for every blessed reality. In that explanation, the Church makes it clear that it is only God that man and angels are bound to give the highest form of worship referred to as Latria. While Hyper dulia, which is a higher form of honour should be directed to the Blessed Virgin Mary, dulia is the proper form of honour to both the saints and the angels, irrespective of their status.

Presently, Theology and her scholars hardly emphasize the existence or otherwise of such articles of faith as purgatory, indulgence, sacramental, grace, angels and demons, as they used to be in pre-Vatican II. But on the other hand, it is apparent that while some pastors of whatever affiliation, continue to make random loosing, casting, binding and pursuing of some demons of all age grade, the issue of the existence of their good partners, the angels, are rarely made a matter of. It is strongly observed that the older faithful hold on to these articles of faith than the younger faithful. Perhaps it is because of the air of **Vatican Council I,** which the older faithful had, but which eluded the younger generation entirely. The church does not tell us to disregard either the angels or the contents of their messages. After the message delivered to Mary by the Archangel, Gabriel, the former accepted both the angel and the content of the message he delivered with strong faith. Today, the Church continues to make that encounter between the angel and the Blessed Virgin Mary a positive strong point of reference. What we should however note is, that neither the Church nor God has located a tangible place to the angels or to the demons.

The importance of this chapter is to make us know whether in confidence, we should confide in angels as good confidants. In the Old Testament, Son of God, is a title given to the angels, the chosen people, the children of Israel, and the kings. It signifies an adoptive sonship that establishes a relationship of a particular intimacy between God and his creatures.

The problems which we have already attempted their answer is, who or what are the angels? We have seen them as disembodied benevolent or malevolent spirits. Angels are pure spirits since they have no flesh and no blood. They are as weightless as phantoms or ghosts which can be defined as something that is invisible, having no flesh, neither can they be heard or be touched. In the **Chapters of Life,** Rampa says that, *A ghost is a person who has apparent breath, thickness, and height, but it is of somewhat shadowy substance, as shadowy as shadow in fact.* [8]

Maybe it is better to say, like Rampa, that angels are a reality that has apparent breadth, thickness, and height, somehow shadowy, but somehow not a person. In his own time the angelic doctor, St. Thomas Aquinas and some of his contemporaries used to conceive and speak of Angels as what used to be human-like, but which however can be in millions, dancing on the tip of a pin or singing in a container which can be as small as your tea cup. The amazing thing about Angelic reality is not just the seemingly multitude of their numbers in a small space, irrespective of their apparent appearances, but the fact that they are penetrable. The hosts of angels and the choirs of angels are expressions that are quite outstanding in the description of their numbers in multitudes, colony and motility; even when they mingle with or without our seeing them. This makes it clearer for us to note that, the number of angels is not the most important point under consideration for now. The Letter to the **Hebrews 12:22,** speaks of "an innumerable company of angels." When his enemies trapped Elisha and his servant, for the sake of his servant who was afraid, the prophet asked God to reveal to the servant the innumerable hosts of angels, that were waiting in the surrounding mountain. Before his crucifixion, Christ asked his tormentors, "do you think that I cannot appeal to my Father, who would promptly send more that twelve regions of angels to my defense?" **(Matt. 26:53).**

What we should bear in mind is not how the Church views the number of angels and their nature as such, but what they think about their reality as a whole. St Augustine gives more clue to both their nature and their behaviour. After his acceptance of their reality, he said that, *Angel is the name of their office, not of their nature. If you seek the name of their nature, it is 'spirit,' from what they do, 'angel.' With their whole beings, the angels are servants and messengers of God*" **(CCC 329).**

The description of angels as servants and messengers, no doubt gives us the picture of a king who is being surrounded by his menservants and maidservants at his beck and call. This ideology is not only in Christianity. In African Traditional Religion (ATR), there is always the concept of the Supreme Being, whom the believer sees as the all knowing and all powerful, and who is reasonably catapulted far away from his creation. But that does not mean that he is totally cut off from that his creation according to that belief.

> We must note that spirit and ancestor worship
> contains certain elements of truth.
> Its instinct is fulfilled in the cult of the Angels
> and Saints. Moreover, it must be pointed out
> that the pagans generally do not believe that
> it is the dumb images as such that they are
> worshipping. Their belief is that there are
> some invisible spirits or powers superior
> to mortal man which actually or virtually
> recede in these images and receive them. [9]

Thus, for the pagans, the role of the deities is to convey man's problems and offences to the Supreme Being in his secret dwelling place, and take his message back to man through the mediation of his angels and priests. We should note that the Jewish, Islamic and Christian religions believe that God makes use of his angels as the king makes use of his emissaries.

The opening words which begin the comments about Archangel Michael, as one of the three Archangels whose remembrance day falls on 29th September states that, *Today the church cerebrates the principal feast in honour of St Michael the Archangel...*[10] In speaking about the guardian angels whose day of honour is October 2nd, the same reference states that,

> The Church honours especially today the Choir of Angels, the innumerable host of spirits whose duties comprise the eternal praising of God, the adoration of the Blessed Sacrament upon earth, the escorting of our Lady, and serving as Guardian Angels to all souls on earth and in purgatory.[11]

The amazing thing about the Church and angelic reality today is the fact that the church hardly emphasizes the role of that holy reality. Below are some fragments of how the Church views the angels in ages past.

THE ARCHANGELS
Archangel Michael

"The early Christians entrusted to St. Michael the care of the Sick. All who bathed in his medical spring near Colossae, and invoked him and the Holy Trinity, were healed; and near Constantinople, the sick used to spend the night in his church in the hope of a cure. Catholic tradition assigns to him the following four offices: To fight against Satan, to rescue the souls of the faithful from his grasp, especially at the hour of death, to be the special Patron of Holy Church, and bring men's souls to judgment."[12]

Archangel Raphael

Apart from the account of the curing of Tobias from his blindness and acting as guide during his son's trip to Meria, the Archangel Raphael as a consequence, has been "...revered as the Patron Saint of travelers, of the young and the innocent. Today's gospel identifies him with the angel who used to come down at certain intervals to stir the water in the probatica pool, which caused the cure of the first invalid who descended into the moving waters."[13]

Archangel Gabriel

The Archangel Gabriel whose name occurred in the Bible and in the Liturgy is mentioned as one of the seven angels who "stand before God." And in a special way, he seems to be the messenger of glad and consoling tidings. He is known as the "angel of annunciation." Although the Church does not seem to have any attributive roles for him, in Jewish tradition, Gabriel was taken to be the angel of judgment as at Sodom, and against the army of Sennecherib; and it is he who was supposed to mark the foreheads of the elect. Christian tradition also attributes to St. Gabriel the message given to the Shepherds at Bethlehem, to St. Joseph in connection with the flight of the Holy Family into Egypt and believes it was he who "strengthened" our Lord in the garden of olives on the night of his betrayal.

It is to be noted here, however, that Mohammed considered Archangel Gabriel, that is Jibril, as the head of all the angels, and claimed that he received his revelation from him.

The Holy Church teaches us that Angels were the first creation. She also teaches us that they are spiritual beings, who are immeasurably superior to man in natural gifts. It is believed that they were called upon to adore the sacred humanity of Jesus Christ, when this was revealed to them before time. While the beatific vision and an intimate union was the reward of the humility of the faithful angels, Lucifer and his followers who rebelled and refused to obey, were cast out of heaven.

> And now war broke out in heaven, when
> Michael with his angels attacked the dragon.
> The dragon fought back with his angels, but

they were defeated and driven out of heaven. The great dragon, the primeval serpent, known as the devil or Satan, who had led all the world astray, was hurled down to the earth and his angels were hurled down with him. Rev. 12:7-9.

Following the notion of bishops and archbishops, Pope St. Gregory in writing about angelic reality noted that,

...no way can they always be called "angels" or "messengers" since they are angels only when something is announced through them. Those who make minor announcements are called angels, those who make important announcements are called archangels."[14]

Moved by his belief in the holy beings, St. Jerome said, "so sublime is the dignity of the soul that from its birth there is appointed to each one a guardian spirit."[15]

I may not have professed to be a devotee of the society of *"Opus Angelorum,"* but so far, what I have said might prove me otherwise and set me even above the members. There are countless witnesses as to what the holy angels have done for the good of the children of God as there are countless number of Angels. The Bible is littered with the exemplary proofs of the reality of the angels and the roles they played too. St. Thomas Aquinas, St. Augustine, St. Bernard, St. Jerome, St. Clement, St. Francis Xavier, St. Gregory the Great are some of the Fathers of the Church whose testimony about the angels would make us long for nothing less than a glance of that reality. St. Memrad, St. Margaret of Cortona, St. Gertrude, St. Denis, St. Catherine of Siena, St. Frances of Rome, St. Rose of Lima and St. Gemma of Galgani are wonderful saints of the past, whose testimonies about the angels should rather make us be concerned about the holy beings than wasting more efforts in binding and casting out the devil. Amazed at the plenitude of the glory of God manifested in the angels, it is said that, "Though we are children and the road that lies ahead of us is so long, and not only long but dangerous, what have we to fear with such guardians? They cannot be vanquished, nor led astray, still less can they lead us astray, these beings who guard us in all our ways. They are faithful, they are wise, they are powerful; what have we to fear? Let us but follow them and cling to them, and we shall abide in the shadow of the Almighty."[16]

In a further consoling piece of Theology, the church reminds us that, "From intimacy to death human life is surrounded by their watchful care and intercession. Beside each believer stands an angel as protector and shepherd leading him to life." (CCC 336)

What the faithful should bear in mind with the guardian angels at their banner include:

i) Angels have very vital roles to play in the maintenance of the order of God's universe. Because they are intelligent, spiritual, powerful and resourceful realities, they are given different kinds of role to play in order to preserve both the visible and invisible order.

ii) They are very serious spiritual forces who direct the order of corporeal beings of man. This is because like Christ's resurrected body, the bodies of angels move between heaven and earth with tremendous ease and velocity.

iii) Angels can become visible according to situation. Remember that they appeared to the shepherds, to Paul during the

59

iv) shipwreck, to Mary, to Christ on the Mountain, to Philip before the conversion of the Ethiopian Eunuch, and even to countless others in the Old Testament.

iv) The inference to the angel and their activities, the destruction and devastation, as well as the restoration and the maintenance of the order of the created order of the world should convince us to have more faith in their reality and the reality of the existence of God.

CHAPTER FOUR
THE HOLY ANGELS ARE OUR BEST FRIENDS

*The great virtue in life is real courage, that knows
how to face facts and live beyond them.*
-D. H. Lawrence

Angels are created beings that respond to God's call and will as guardians, helpers, protectors, messengers who are sent wherever they are needed to go. Gideon's army of 300 destroyed thousands of Syrian soldiers during the night because of the ambassadorial function of the angels. Men of God were led and directed by the angels in the past.

"Now when Joshua was near Jericho, he looked up and saw a man standing in front of him, grasping a naked sword. Joshua walked towards him and said to him, 'Are you on our side or on that of our enemies?' He replied, 'On neither side. I have come now as the captain of army of Yahweh.' Joshua fell on his face to the ground, worshipping him, and said, 'what has my Lord to say to his servant?' The captain of the army of Yahweh answered, 'Take your sandals off your feet, for the place where you are standing is holy.'" **Joshua 5: 13-15.**

Although an angel appeared to Joshua, the passage shows that the angel in question did not come to favour Joshua and the people of Israel or to favour their enemies; but perhaps to show that God protects even our enemies as he protects us. It was when their sin reached the highest that the Lord withdrew his protection from the People of Sodom and Gomorrah. The destruction of the city took place immediately the feet of the Angels and the feet of Abraham took leave of the boundaries of the city. Saul, though an individual, just like Judas Iscariot in the New Testament, began to suffer the loss of the glory of God in his life because of his persistence in pride and deliberate alienation of himself from the grip of the Spirit of the Lord. What of course we should note is that God's protection is always over and around us through various means; and it is only our persistent and arrogant stay in sin can force him to withdraw his favour and protection from us. During their sojourn in Egypt, God who protected the people of Israel knew that their protection depended on their obedience to what he told them, He advised them on what they should do, after which he warned them thus, "If I see the blood I will pass over you." And so, it came to be that the angel of the Lord protected the Israelites.

The summary account of God's protection of his people through the agency of his holy angels can be seen as below within the context of the roles of the angelic creatures.

Cherubim and Seraphim.

These two group of spiritual beings are known to guard the throne of God, to guard his sanctuary, adore him and sing before his presence without end. In **Genesis 3:24,** we read, "so he drove out the man; and He placed at the east end of the garden of Eden Cherubim, and a flaming sword which turned every way, to guard the way to the tree of life." And to show the pre-eminence of the glory of God above every other thing, the Cherubim will be the symbol which will be used to make the Ark of the Covenant. And Moses was instructed to follow the exact pattern of the heavenly reality, in making the ark. **Ex. 25:18-20.** Cherubim like the Seraphim also have wings. Although they have human features, they have but an imaginary picture of a man with wings. In Isaiah chapter six, the Seraphim are defined as "fiery ones", having as much as six wings, and known for their burning love for God in adoration of his holiness.

Angels of Churches.

From the revelation of St. John, we come to know that God never leaves His Church without the protection of his angels. From the words, "To the angel of the Church at Ephesus write...," we can rightly infer that other Churches that are not the Church of Ephesus, have also protecting angels and their protection is no less strong than it is in those of the Churches of Thyatira, Smyrna, Pergamos, Sardis, Philadelphia and Laodicea.

Angels of Judgment

Perhaps the earthly roles of the angels will come to climax at the judgment of the world, and may even end there, for verse one of the sixteenth chapter of Apocalypse reads, "Then I heard a loud voice from the sanctuary calling to the seven angels, 'Go, and empty the seven bowels of God's anger over the earth.'" And when Christ was speaking, he said, "Go away from me, with your curse upon you, to the eternal fire prepared for the devil and his angels." **Matt. 25:41.**

64

From common sense experience, kings always have the services of their servants at their beck and call. Every family has formal or paraformal division of labour. From the beginning of every activity to its completion, there is always something to be done; indeed something to be done by the proper personnel. I always remember how our headmaster used to instruct us, "sweep the classrooms, pick the pieces of paper, dust the blackboard, set the seats and tables before you come out for the assembly." Even before the announcement of our end of term results and our certification, the same good old headmaster would announce to us through the teachers, the same instructions he gives to us before our morning assemblies. What the headmaster was to us his pupils at the beginning, during and at the end of the academic session, is what Christ is to us through the angels at the beginning during and at the end of the world.

Before the final gathering and the ingathering of the children of God, the angels of God would sweep off the evil doers from the stock of the

good people. They would also put in their order, every other odds and ends in creation, before the Lord in his glory appears with his rewards in the company of the holy angels. Thus the angels of judgment carry out their activities by chastising, rebuking and exhorting people by way of warning to the world about the impending doom.

Revelation (16:4-5), states that, "The third angel emptied his bowel into the rivers and springs of water and they turned into blood. Soon after that, I saw an angel standing in the sun, and he shouted aloud to all the birds that were flying high overhead in the sky, 'Come here! Gather together at God's great feast.' **19:17.** And when the dust of the warning have settled, "the angels will appear and separate the wicked from the upright, to throw them into the blazing furnace, where there will be weeping and grinding of teeth."
Matt. 13:49. "At the signal given by the voice of the Archangel and the trumpet of God, the Lord himself will come down from heaven; those who have died in Christ will be the first to rise, and only after that shall we who remain alive be taken up in the clouds, together with them, to meet the Lord in the air."**1 Thess. 4:16**

CHAPTER FIVE
THE GUARDIANSHIP OF THE HOLY ANGELS

Make the holy Angels your friends! No matter how weak you may be, how sad your condition, or how great the perils which surround us, we have nothing to fear under the protection of such guardians! - St. Bernard

In our own time, angels are still what they were before the creation of man, before the coming of Christ, and in fact, during the time of Christ. The Philosopher, Leibniz, argued that, there were many possible worlds, each having all the possible properties that suited it. And when he was expounding his thought further, he argued that there were many possible Judases too, and each of the possible worlds has its own Judas that would help to bring about the salvation of its own possible people. Although the same logic may not seem to be appropriate in the context of discuss on angels here, yet the roles of the holy angels, through history, have brought about the safety of man, and to some extent, the salvation of his soul, especially when and only if man hearkened to the voice of the Lord.

Sometimes, when we are alone and meditative, we feel as if there is someone around us, though we cannot explain how. Sometimes too when we remain alone, we feel great and powerful, though we may be in hostile and fearful environment. Often too, we marvel at how we were able to overcome certain precarious situations and environments. That shows that we have the sense and the feeling that there is something or somebody seeing us through. After the mishap of Tsunami, a little boy was dug out alive from a portion of the incidence after many days. In the scene of many ghastly accidents, people marvelled at the fact that somebody or people came out alive from the ill-fated vehicle or even airplane. The plane crash that took place in Ogun State of Nigeria by the mid 2006, which claimed not less than hundred lives, took the lives of the likes of Alhaji Maccido, the Sultan of Sokoto caliphate, and his two daughters. Yet, nine people came out alive from that plane that battered to bits and pieces. After the ghastly motor accident that involved me at Ibusa of Delta State, in March 2002, a good Catholic who was a witness to the incident said that the bang of the two cars that were involved in the dangerous accident was horrific. And

about me, he added, "His angel is really alive."
It was after a few minutes in the state of no
where, or what you call unconsciousness, that

the scene, the two cars and the accident made
me believe that the Lord has done it for me, in
a way that I could not explain even today.
Thus, only the eye witnesses from the adjacent
filling station can tell the convincing story that
the two people in the other car, and the three
of us in ours were all alive after all. Perhaps a
favourable day would come when my friends
will come together for a more wonderful
thanksgiving, even as it is advised that
Christians should occasionally offer
thanksgiving to the Lord for His ever-fatherly
protection from all forms of danger.

In the words of the Psalm we read, no disaster
can overtake you, no plague come near your
tent; he has given his angels orders about you,
to guard you wherever you go.
They will carry you in their arms, in case you
trip over a stone, You will walk upon a wild
beast and adder, you will trample young lions
and snakes. **(Psalm. 91:10-13).**

69

When those things said in the Psalm take place, those who have faith do know. And it is possible that they appreciate the Lord's protection in their lives; but how, they cannot say. In that situation, what we only say as the

good children of God is that, "The Lord has done it for me!" And in our popular language, we call it miracle. Perhaps, miracles follow mysteries. It might be better to summarize as mysterious every mishap that comes our way, and as miraculous whatever means the Lord has used in saving us.

We do not of course rule out the guardianship and the constant role of the protection of our guardian angels. Those who have faith also believe so. What we know of is that to see the angels with our human eyes is only a privilege to a given few, lest we begin to take them common; or the devil seizes that opportunity to deceive more people. Some of the saints however had the privilege to see and even interact with their guardian angel. St. Catherine of Siena is one of those saints so favoured. The story about her interaction with her guardian angel relates that in her lifetime, St. Catherine was once praying, but she was distracted and looked away at that instant.

What she saw in the direction of her distraction was her guardian angel, who gave her a reprimanding look for her disrespect in the presence of the Most Holy God. And to make amend for this, the little saint made a severe penance for that little stroke of slothfulness. St Francis de Sales relates a story about a newly ordained priest and a little piece of drama with his guardian angel. According to the Saint, he noticed that a young priest, soon after his ordination to the priesthood, hesitated before he passed through doors as if he meant to let in someone first. When St. Francis asked the priest, "Why do you pause?" The priest answered thus, "God favours me with the sight of my Guardian Angel. Before I was ordained to the holy priesthood, my Angel always remained at my right and preceded me. Now, he walks at the left and refuses to go before me."[17] Perhaps this gesture further proves the inferiority of the angelic state to that of the priesthood of Christ, in which the priest partakes. This further confirms the words of the scripture which says, "Let all the angels of God pay him homage." **Heb. 1:6.** When St. Rose of Lima was growing up, she was privileged to have conversations in familiar matters with her Holy Angels. She was of course on several occasions delivered from danger and serious difficulties. In fact, it was said, that she once said that her guardian angel did whatever she wanted him to do. However, what she wanted him to do of course must have to be godly things. It was reported that his guardian angel favoured the great Pope, who became the great St. Gregory, with his Papal status, because he developed special love for him as an infant. When he was the abbot of a monastery, which he built in Rome, the guardian angel of the saint frequented him, disguised as a poor merchant begging for alms. And when he became Pope, the saint, Gregory, began the method of feeding twelve poor mendicants every day. On the process, he discovered one of the beggars who had extraordinary virtues that impressed him very much. When he interacted with that virtuous beggar, he told him in reply that, "I am the poor merchant to whom you gave, besides twelve dollars, the silver dish of your mother. This act of charity which I caused you to perform prepared you for the dignity of High Priest. I am your Angel. Fear not, Gregory. God sent me to tell you that you would obtain everything you asked for through my service. As I was the cause of your being raised to the Chair of St. Peter, I shall also protect and preserve you in this position until death." [18]

The word of God reminds us to continue to love each other as brothers, and remember always to welcome strangers, for by doing this, some people have entertained angels without knowing it. **Heb 13:2.**

We can go on and on narrating about the saints and their guardian angels. This does not mean that those who are not saints are not so favoured with the vision of the angels, even their guardian angels. No, people are still so favoured even today, but the problem is that those who are so inclined to dedication and devotion, especially to the holy angels lessens day by day; for it is only "The clean of heart and pure of heart " **Psalm 24:4,** that will see God and his angels. **Matt. 5:8.** If having clean hands and pure heart implies having the vision of God and those of the Holy angels, as we have seen in the lives of the saints, then the other way may be the reason why more Christians in this our sinful and wicked generation see demons and evil spirits. That means that in the past, while there was stronger devotion to the holy angels, much efforts is directed towards detecting and casting out devils by the present generation. But this does not mean that the function of the

73

angels as our protectors has changed or has ceased. READER'S DIGEST of August 1988, carried a sweet story with the sharp heading that read, **The Boy, the Snake and an Angel.** The story was about a young Florida boy, who was hunting with his dog with an air riffle. In pursuit of a game, the boy jumped across a ditch only to land on a peaceful rattlesnake, which struck the fangs into the boy's shoe and could not work itself free. At that, the boy's dog finally bit the snake's head off and set the snake free. However the boy's foot was full of venom and worse, one of the fangs had entered a vein. The effect of this was immediate and very painful too. The boy became dizzy and knew he could not make home his way, 150 yards away, over the rough terrain. He lost all consciousness. However, after many days, when he had regained his consciousness, he told his surprising story which said that before he lost consciousness, an individual in white robe appeared, held him up and carried him to their house where his mother found him unconscious. The stranger told him that he would be very sick, but that he would recover. Then, the *angel* disappeared. The boy said that he thought that he saw God.

Christ said that his father goes on working, so does He; so do the angels and all other good categories that God causes to work, and so should we till the end of time. If the angels prevented the first parents from eating of the fruit of the tree of life, lest they die, we have reason to hope that they will even protect us from unforeseen dangers, and even death. If the angels of God led the people of Israel on their journey, we must be convinced that the angels, both in groups and individuals will lead us to safety, when we are traveling by sea, by land, by air, and even in our sleep. In the lives of Adam and Eve, Isaac, Joshua, Manoah, Abraham, Noah, Lot, Tobit and his son; even Mary, Peter and Paul in the New Testament, we read about the saving role of the Holy Angels leading man to salvation. Therefore, we should be convinced that in the lives of Okoye, Kofi, Ngugi, Okani, Ampho, and even Nnenne, Onochie and Moi, you and me, the angel of God is on guard about us carrying out the protective assignment that God gave them. God is ever faithful, he never stops to guide us his children, and he easily does it through the instrumentality of the guardian angels.

We owe a duty to God and to our dear Angels.

Whether or not we are privileged to touch the angels of God, feel their smell, or interact with them or see them is not as important as how in faith we believe in their existence. we must also avoid neglecting and offending God through our sinfulness and lack of faith. We should always bear in mind that we are not expected to worship the angels. The type of reverence the angels need from us is dulia. As pure instruments of goodness, angels of God are very much at home with us when we are in the state of grace and when we are doing the will of God. When we were very young, we were told that even our confessions make our angels to be ashamed of us if we make bad confessions; in such a situation, he covers his face and keeps his distance. But on the other hand, he closes on us if we do good confessions. But confessions apart, what we know is that our guardian angels are good lovers of the Blessed Sacrament, uprightness, constant contrition and godly dispositions. Therefore we are very much disposed to receive their guiding protection if we live godly lives, especially the life of prayer and seeking the face of God, and being obedient to the angels. "Look, I am sending an angel to precede you, to guard you as you go and bring you to the place that I have prepared. Revere him and obey what he says." **Ex. 23:20.**

The life of impurity, state of sin, as well as abhorrence of prayer, infidelity is what displeases our guardian angels the most. These days, there is more sense of infidelity, apostasy, neo-peganism and syncretism, among Christians. These negative attitudes towards God and goodness leave the angels of God at arms length.
Nevertheless, since they are carrying out God's command over us, angel of God hardly leaves even the sinner to himself so long the sinner is still in this sinful world. He only leaves man to himself, as it was the case of Saul and Judas, when man out of pride, irremediably sins against the Holy Spirit, in the form of final impenitence. Otherwise, "the Guardian Angels preserve both our souls and bodies from all manner of danger. They defend us when we are tempted by evil spirits, and especially at the hour of death; they inspire holy thoughts and deeds in God's service; they warn us of impending spiritual dangers, and carry our prayer to the throne of God, united with their own; finally, they conduct our souls into purgatory and bring them to heaven when all

faults have been fully expiated. Only at the judgment seat of God is their task completed."[19]

PART THREE

TO GOD THROUGH THE ANGELS

ANGELS: *OUR UNSEEN PROTECTORS*

"They will carry you in their arms in case you trip over a stone." Psalm 91:12

INTRODUCTION TO THE CONSECRATION TO THE GUARDIAN ANGEL

This consecration brings about a more wide spread veneration of the Angels, especially to the Guardian Angel. It is completely voluntary and offered to those who feel drawn to it. Those who wish to enter into a closer bond with the Guardian Angel will see in it the fulfillment of a secret longing to be more closely united with the Angels.

This consecration is, in reality, nothing else than an open confession of one's adherence to God, to Mary, the Mother of God, to the Church and to one's Guardian Angel.

The consecration to the Guardian Angel can be made by any Christian, irrespective of age and profession, as soon as he is able to understand its meaning, sincerely venerates his Angel and is ever willing, to experience his assistance more and more.

The consecration is made within the framework of a little ceremony, before or after benediction or individually before a priest. There are no obligations in the form of daily prayers. A good intimate relationship with one's Guardian Angel, however, should be fostered and developed. As a rule, the formula of consecration should be written and signed by the candidate himself and be handed to the priest after the consecration. It is the ecclesiastical document of an action which draws down the divine blessing and the protection of Mary, Queen of the Angels. The rite and act of consecration has the approval of the Church.

In order to give children also the opportunity of making this consecration to the Guardian Angel a special formula is provided, in which god parents and the mother substitute before God and ask for the protection and sure guidance of the Guardian Angel.

In schools, at the beginning of the scholastic year, a promise to the Guardian Angel may be made. It can also be taken in the month of September, popularly known as the month of the Guardian Angels. This, however, is not regarded as an acceptance into the Work of the Angels, but as a missionary aid to provide children with a strong spiritual help.

81

CONSECRATION TO THE GUARDIAN ANGEL

(With ecclesiastical approval by the Apostolic
Administration of Innsbruck, 14.2.1951)

[This Consecration should be made before
the Blessed Sacrament]

Come, Holy Spirit, Creator, come
From your bright heavenly throne,
Come take possession of our souls
And make them all your own.

You who are called the Paraclete
Best gift of God above,
The living spring, the living fire
Sweet unction and true love.

You who are sevenfold in your grace,
Finger of God's right hand;
His promise teaching "little ones
To speak and understand.

Guide our minds with your blessed light,
With love our hearts inflame,
And with your strength which ne'er decays
Confirm our mortal frame.

Far from us drive our deadly foe;
True peace unto us bring
And through all perils tead us safe
Beneath your sacred wing.

Through you may we the Father know,
Through you the Eternal Son,
And you the Spirit of them both
Thrice-blessed Three in One.

All glory to the Father be
With his co-equal Son!
The same to you great Paraclete,
While endless ages run.
Amen.

Priest:
Lord and God, in the knowledge of our own misery and unworthiness and only relying on the intercession of our heavenly Mother Mary, our holy Guardian Angel and all the Angels and Saints, we come to you and ask you humbly not to remember our sins.

Candidate:
I confess to almighty God, and to you my brothers and sisters, that I have sinned through my own fault in my thoughts and in my words,

in what I have done, and in what I have failed to do; and I ask blessed Mary, ever Virgin, all the Angels anq Saints, and you, my brothers and sisters, to pray for e to the Lord our God.

Priest:

May almighty God have mercy on us, forgive us our sins, and bring us to everlasting life. Amen.

Priest (continues):

Most holy Virgin Mary and Mother of God! You are the Queen and Mistress of all the Angels, and, therefore, also of our Guardian Angels. Here before our Lord and God, before all the Angels and Saints, we desire to commit ourselves entirely to our Guardian Angel and to unite ourselves closely to him.

Candidate:

(Recites now the Consecration, kneeling and holding a burning candle).

Holy Guardian Angel, who have been given to me from the beginning of my life as my Guardian and Companion.

I, poor sinner... desire to consecrate myself to you before my Lord and God, my heavenly

84

Mother Mary and all the Angels and Saints. I wish to unite myself closely to you forever.

In this union I promise always to be loyal and obedient to my God and Lord and to our holy Mother the Church.

I promise always to acknowledge Mary as my Mistress, Queen and Mother and to imitate her way of life.

I promise to acknowledge you always as my holy Guardian and to promote, as much as lies in my power, the veneration of the holy Angels as the protection and the help which is given to us in a very special way in these days of spiritual combat for the Kingdom of God.

I beg you, holy Angel of God, obtain for me a love so strong that I may be inflamed by it, a faith so firm that I may never falter. I beg you to assist me against the assaults of the enemy. I beg you for the grace of Mary's humility so that I may escape all dangers and, guided by you, may reach the gates of our heavenly home. Amen.

Priest:

Lord, Almighty God, may the gift of our consecration and the intercession of our holy Guardian Angels be pleasing in your sight. May those whom we venerate on earth be our advocates with you in heaven. Through our Lord Jesus Christ your Son, who with you and the Holy Spirit lives and reigns one God, for ever. Amen.

P. CONFIRM, O Lord, what you have wrought in us
C. From your holy temple, which is in Jerusalem.
P. SAVE your servants and your handmaids,
C. Who put their trust in you, my God
P. SEND your aid, O Lord, from on high
C. And from Zion watch over us.
P. O LORD, hear my prayer j
C. And let my cry come to you.
P. The Lord be with you
C. And also with you.

Let us pray:

O God, who in a wonderful way have established the ministry of Angels, and of men, mercifully grant that your holy Angels who are ever serving you in heaven, may also be our protectors here on earth. Through Christ our Lord. Amen.

My soul glorifies the Lord.
My spirit rejoices in God, my Saviour.
He looks on his servant in her nothingness;
Henceforth all ages will call me blessed.

The Almighty works marvels for me.
Holy His name!
His mercy is from age to age
On those who fear him.

He puts forth his arm in strength
And scatters the proud hearted.
He casts the mighty from their thrones
And raises the lowly.

He fills the starving with good things,
Sends the rich away empty.
He protects Israel, his servant,
Remembering his mercy,
the mercy promised to our fathers
For Abraham and his sons for ever.
Glory be to the Father...

LET US PRAY:

Lord mercifully send us your holy Angel. May he, who is always in your presence, as our faith teaches us, bring our prayers before you that you may bless them. Receive them gra/ciously through the intercession of the holy Angels and may they obtain for us salvation. Through Christ our Lord. Amen.

LITANY OF THE HOLY GUARDIAN ANGEL
(For private use only)

Lord, have mercy on us.
Christ, have mercy on us.
Lord, have mercy on us, Christ, hear us.
Christ, graciously hear us.
God the Father of Heaven,
Have mercy on us.
God the Son, Redeemer of the world,
Have mercy on us.
God the Holy Ghost,
Have mercy on us.
Holy Trinity, One God,
Have mercy on us.

Holy Mary, Queen of the Angels, *pray for us.*
Holy Angel, my guardian, *pray for us.*
Holy Angel, my prince,
Holy Angel, my monitor,
Holy Angel, my counselor,
Holy Angel, my defender,   "   "   "
Holy Angel, my steward,
Holy Angel, my friend,
Holy Angel, my negotiator,
Holy Angel, my intercessor,
Holy Angel, my patron,
Holy Angel, my director,

89

Holy Angel, my ruler,   " " "
Holy Angel, my protector,
Holy Angel, my comforter,
Holy Angel, my brother,
Holy Angel, my teacher,
Holy Angel, my shepherd,
Holy Angel, my witness,
Holy Angel, my helper,
Holy Angel, my watcher,
Holy Angel, my conductor,
Holy Angel, my preserver,
Holy Angel, my instructor,
Holy Angel, my enlightener,

Lamb of God, Who takest away the sins of the world,
Spare us, O Lord.
Lamb of God, Who takest away the sins of the world,
Graciously hear us, O Lord.
Lamb of God, Who takest away the sins of the world,
Have mercy on us.
Christ, hear us.
Christ, graciously hear us.

V. Pray for us, O holy Guardian Angel,
R. That we may be made worthy of the promises of Christ.

Let Us Pray

Almighty and everlasting God, Who in the counsel of Thine ineffable goodness hast appointed to all the Faithful, from their mother's womb, a special Angel Guardian of their body and soul, grant that I may so love and honor him whom Thou hast so mercifully given me that, protected by the bounty of Thy grace and by his assistance, I may merit to behold with him and all the angelic hosts, the glory of Thy countenance in the heavenly kingdom, Thou Who livest and reignest world without end. R. Amen.

Novena Prayer
*(A novena is made by praying a prayer
for nine days in succession.)*

O HOLY ANGEL, whom God, by the effect of His goodness and His tender regard for my welfare, has charged with the care of my conduct, and who assists me in all my wants and comforts me in all my afflictions, who supports me when I am discouraged and continually obtains for me new favors, I return thee profound thanks, and I earnestly beseech thee, O most amiable protector, to continue thy

91

charitable care and defense of me against the malignant attacks of all my enemies. Keep me away from all occasions of sin. Obtain for me the grace of listening attentively to thy holy inspirations and of faithfully putting them into practice. In particular, I implore thee to obtain for me the favor which I ask for by this novena. (Here mention your petition.) Protect me in all the temptations and trials of this life, but more especially at the hour of my death, and do not leave me until thou hast conducted me into the presence of my Creator in the mansions of everlasting happiness. Amen.

Angel of God

ANGEL OF GOD, my Guardian dear, To whom His love commits me here, Ever this day (or night) be at my side,
To light and guard, to rule and guide. Amen.

Prayer to Our Guardian Angel

O HOLY Guardian Angel, my dear friend and solicitous guide on the dangerous way of life, to thee be heartfelt thanks for the numberless benefits which have been granted me through thy love and goodness and for the powerful help by which thou hast preserved me from so many dangers and temptations. I beg of thee, let me further experience thy love and thy care. Avert from me all danger, increase in me horror for sin and love for all that is good. Be a counselor and consoler to me in all the affairs of my life, and when my life draws to a close, conduct my soul through the valley of death into the kingdom of eternal peace, so that in eternity we may together praise God and rejoice in His glory. Through Jesus Christ Our Lord. Amen.

O Angel of God, make me worthy of thy tender love, thy celestial companionship and thy never-failing protection!

Prayer for a Happy Death
By St. Charles Boromeo

IN THE NAME of the Most Holy Trinity, Father, Son and Holy Ghost, I, a poor, unhappy sinner, make this solemn declaration before thee, O beloved Angel, who has been given me as a protector by the Divine Majesty:

1. I desire to die in the Faith which the Holy, Roman and Apostolic Church adhere to and defends, in which all the Saints of the New

Testament have died. I pray thee, provide that I may not depart out of this life before the Holy Sacraments of that Church have been administered to me.

2. I pray that I may depart from this life under thy holy protection and guidance, and I beseech thee, therefore, to assist me at the hour of my death and to propitiate the Eternal Judge, whose Sacred Heart was inflamed with most ardent love for sinners upon the Cross.

3. With my whole heart I long to be made a partaker of the merits of Jesus Christ and His holy Mother Mary, thine exalted Queen, and I pray thee, through the sufferings of Jesus on the Cross, to mitigate the agonies of my death and to move the Queen of Heaven to cast her loving glance upon me, a poor sinner, in that dreadful hour, for my sweetest consolation.

O my dearest Guardian Angel! Let my soul be placed in thy charge, and when it has gone forth from the prison of this body, do thou deliver it into the hands of its Creator and Redeemer, that with thee and all the Saints, it may gaze upon Him in the bliss of Heaven, love Him perfectly and find its blessedness in Him throughout eternity. Amen.

Good Night Prayer
GOOD NIGHT, my Guardian Angel,
The day has sped away;
Well spent or ill, its story
Is written down for aye.

And now, of God's kind Providence,
Thou image pure and bright,
Watch o'er me while I'm sleeping--
My Angel dear, good night!

Ejaculations
Hail, glorious Angel, appointed by God to be my guardian!
Hail, holy Angel, my protector in all dangers!
Hail, holy Angel, my defense in all afflictions!
Hail, holy Angel, my most faithful friend!
Hail, holy Angel, my guide!
Hail, holy Angel, my preceptor!
Hail, holy Angel, witness of all my actions!
Hail, holy Angel, my helper in every difficulty!
Hail, holy Angel, my counselor in doubt!
Hail, holy Angel, my shield at the hour of death!

PRAYER TO MICHAEL, THE ARCHANGEL

Glorious Prince of the Celestial host, O Michael the archangel, defend us in the conflict which we have to sustain "against Principalities and power against the world rulers of darkness, against the spiritual forces, of wickedness on high (Eph. 6: 1 2). Come to the rescue of men who God has created in his image and likeness and whom He has redeemed at a great price, from the tyranny of the devil. It is you whom Holy Church venerates as her guardian and her protector? You whom the Lord has charged to conduct redeemed souls into heaven. Pray, therefore, the God of peace to subdue Satan beneath our feet, that he may no longer retain men captive nor do injury to the Church. Present our prayers to the most high God, that without delay they may draw His mercy down upon us. Seize "the dragon, the old serpent, which is the, devil and Satan," bind him and cast him into the bottomless pit..."that he may no longer seduce the nations. (Apoc 20:20-3)

LITANY OF SAINT MICHAEL
(For private use only)

Lord, have mercy on us,
Lord have mercy on us

Christ, have mercy on us.
Christ, have mercy on us.
Lord, have mercy on us.
Lord have mercy on us
Christ, hear us.
Christ, graciously hear us

God the Father of Heaven,
Have mercy on us.
God the Son, Redeemer of the world,
Have mercy on us.
God the Holy Spirit,
Have mercy on us.
Holy Trinity, One God,
Have mercy on us.
Holy Mary Queen of Angels,   Pray for us
St. Michael,   "   "   "
St. Michael, filled with the wisdom of God,
St. Michael, perfect adorer of the Incarnate Word,
St. Michael, crowned with honour and glory,

97

St. Michael, most powerful Prince of the armies
of the Lord,

St. Michael, standard-bearer of the Most Holy
Trinity

St. Michael, victor over Satan,

St. Michael, guardian of Paradise,

St. Michael, guide and comforter of the people
of Israel,

St. Michael, splendor and fortress of the
Church Militant,

St. Michael, honour and joy of the Church
Triumphant,

St. Michael, light of Angels

St. Michael, but Mark of orthodox believers,

St. Michael, strength of those who fight under
the standard of the Cross.

St, Michael, light and comforter of souls at the
hour of death,

St. Michael, our most sure aid,

St. Michael, our help in all adversities,

St. Michael, Herald of the everlasting sentence,

St. Michael, Consoler of souls detained in the
flames of purgatory.

Thou whom the Lord has charged to receive
souls after death,

St. Michael, our Prince,

St. Michael, our Advocate,

Lamb of God, who takes away the sins of the world,
Spare us, O Lord.
Lamb of God, who take away the sins of the world,
graciously near us O Lord,
Lamb of God who takes away the sins of the world,
Have mercy on us.

Pray for us. Oh glorious St. Michael, Prince of the Church of Jesus Christ,
R. That we may be worthy of His promises.

Let Us Pray:
Sanctify us, we beseech thee, O Lord, with thy holy blessing, and grant us, by the intercession of St. Michael, that wisdom which teaches us to lay up treasures in Heaven by exchanging the goods of this world for those of eternity, You who lives and reigns world without end.
R. Amen.

EXORCISM
In the name of Jesus Christ, our Lord and Saviour, strengthened by the intercession' of the Immaculate Virgin Mary, Mother of God, of (the) Blessed Michael, the Archangel, of the

Blessed Apostles Peter, Paul and all the Saints, and powerful in the holy authority of our ministry we confidently undertake to repulse the attacks and deceits of the devil.

Psalm 67/68
Let God arise, let his enemies be scattered; let them that hate him flee before him. As smoke is driven away so drive them away; as wax melts before the fire so let the wicked perish at the presence of God"

V. Behold the Cross of the Lord, flee bands of enemies.
R. The lion of the Tribe of Judah, the Offspring of David has conquered.
V. May your Mercy, Lord, descend upon us,
R As great as our hope is in you.

We drive you from us, whoever you may be, unclean spirit, satanic powers, infernal invaders, wicked legions, assemblies and sects, in the name and by the virtue of our Lord Jesus Christ may you be snatched away and driven from the church of God and from the souls redeemed by the precious blood of the Divine lamb. Cease your audacity, cunning serpent, to delude the human race, to persecute the Church, to torment God's elect

and to sift them as wheat This is the command made to you by the most high God, with whom in your haughty insolence you still pretend to be his equal,
The God "who wants all men to be saved and come to the knowledge of the truth" (1 Tim. 24).

God trie Father commands you. God the son commands you. God the Holy Spirit commands you. Christ commands you the eternal word of God made flesh, he who to save our race, outdone through your malice, "humbled himself, becoming obedient even unto death" (Phil 2.8). He who has built his Church on firm rock and declared that the gates of hell shall not prevail against her, because he dwells with her all days even to the consummation of the ages".

(Matt. 28.20). The hidden virtue of the cross requires it of you as does also the power of the mysteries of the Christian faith". The glorious Mother of God, "the Virgin Mary commands you, she who by her humility and from the first moment of her immaculate conception crushed your proud head. The faith of the holy apostles Peter and Paul and of the other apostles

command you; the blood of the martyrs and the pious intercession of air, the saints, command you. Thus, you crushed dragon, and you wicked legions, we adjure you by the living God, the true God, by the holy God, by the God "who so loved the world that he delivered his only Son that every soul believing in .him might not perish but have life everlasting". (John 3.16). Cease deceiving human creatures and pouring out to them the poison of eternal perdition; cease harming the Church and hindering her liberty: Retreat, Satan, inventor and master of all deceit, enemy of man's salvation. Cede the' place to the one, Holy, Catholic, and Apostolic Church acquired by Christ at the price of his precious blood. Stoop beneath the all-powerful hand of God. Tremble and flee at the invocation of the holy and powerful name of Jesus, this name which causes hell to tremble, this name to which the virtues, powers and dominations of heaven are humbly submissive, this name which the Cherubim and Seraphim praise unceasingly repeating: Holy, Holy, Holy, is the Lord, the God of Armies.

V. O Lord, hear my prayer
R. And let my cry come to you.

V. The Lord be with you.
R. And also with you.

LET US PRAY

God of heaven, God of earth, God of Angels God of Archangels, God of Patriarchs, God of Prophets, God of Apostles, God of Martyrs, God of Confessors, God of Virgins,

God who has power to give, life after death rest after work; because there is no other God than you and there can be no other, for you are the creator of all things; visible, and invisible; of whose reign there shall be no end, we humbly prostrate ourselves before your glorious majesty and we supplicate you to deliver us from their furious wickedness. Deign, O Lord, to protect us by your power and to preserve us safe and sound. We beseech you through Jesus Christ our Lord. Amen.

From the snares of the devil, deliver us, O Lord that your Church may serve you in peace and liberty; we beseech you to hear us. That you crush down all enemies of your church; we beseech you, hear us. (Holy water is sprinkled in the place where we may be).

REFERENCES

The Encyclopedia of Religion, ed. Mircea Eliade et al., Macmillan Pub. Co., N. Y., 1987 (vol. 1, p. 283)

E. Bolaji Idowu, **African Traditional Religion: A Definition.** SCM Press Ltd., 58 Bloomsbury Street., London, WC 1, 1980, (p.170-171)

Dr. Kalvin K.. Katter, **Angels:** Pub. Bride of Christ International Ltd., P. O. Box 202, Oshodi, Lagos, (p. 57).

William Barclay, **The Daily Study Bible,** Theological Publications in India, Bangalore, 1995, (vol. 8, p. 34)

Jerome Biblical Commentary Ed. Raymond E. Brown S. S. et. Al., Vol. 1 &11; printed in Great Britain by Fletcher & Sons Ltd., Norwich, 1980, (no 13:14).

Dr. Kalvin K.. Katter, **Angels,** p.47

Marcio Souza, **The Order of the Day,** *An Unidentified Flying Opus*, Trans. by Thomas

Colchie, And Pub. In Brazil by Editora Marco Zero Ltd., 1986, (p. xv).

Robsang Rampa, **Chapters of Life**. Pub. By Transworld pub., Century House, 61-63, Uxbridge Road, Ealing, London W5 5SA, 1967, (p. 68).

Our Strange gods, Most Rev. Dr. Godfrey Mary Paul Okoye, Ude's Pub. Co., Ltd., Mgbowo Town, Awgu, Enugu Nigeria., 1965, (p.65).

Saints Companions for Each Day, St. Paul's Pub., Bandra, Bombay, 400 050, 1986, (Sept. 29)

Saints Companions for Each Day, Oct. 2nd

Ibid.

Ibid.

From the **Homilies of Pope St. Gregory the Great on the Gospels.** Hom. 34, 8-9; taken from the 2nd reading of the The Divine office, (Sept. 29).

Saints Companions for Each Day, Oct. 2nd.

Taken from the sermons of St. Bernard, (sermon 12 on Ps 90), *2nd Reading of October 2^{nd,}* in **The Divine Office, vol. III,**

The Guardian Angels, TAN Books and Publishers, Inc., Rockford Illinois 61105, 1956, (p. 43).
Saints Companions for Each Day, Oct. 2nd

Other References

The new Jerusalem Bible, Printed in Great Britain at the University Press, 1985.

The Catechism of the Catholic Church (CCC).

The Divine Office, (The Liturgy of the Hours According to the Roman Rite), 1994.

Dear Reader,

Most of us owe our successes in life on the legacy others left us. Others too, on the quotations, references, influences and in fact experiences and advices from other people who meant well for us. Therefore, to guide our teaming youth, indeed our semiliterate society live more fulfilled life, write me on one or on the following two:

a)   An experience, inspiration, or piece of advice from another person that has helped you in life, stating how, when, (and if possible where), it took place, as well as how it has helped you.

b)   A regrettable experience that seems to have done some harm to you, but with the help of which you have changed for better.

Eg: when Rev. Fr. Dr. Nnoruka was teaching us Modern Philosophy, He quoted Henry Begerson as saying, **"to be alive is to be active."**

In explanation, he said the philosopher meant that it is the person who performs and contributes positively for a better society can be said to be really alive. I there and then decided and began to work to be one of such people.

.... (Your signature)

Rich. N. Ekegbo, a Catholic Priest of Awka Diocese.

Note:

i)   If you wish, indicate the extent you would like your identity to be confidential.

ii)   What you write will just be compiled in a book form along with those of others. No corrections or changes will be effected, because of that, try to make it very short, at most one page.

iii)   The expected last date for this requirement is December, 2009.

iv)   Because of your signature,(and perhaps you would like your contribution to appear in your own hand writing), scan the information into the E-mail:richploughman@yahoo.com or write to box 62, Amawbia, Awka South L.G. A. Anambra State, Nigeria.

THE AUTHOR

Rich N. Ekegbo, who as a priest, has written so many books before **Angels:** *an Unseen Reality,* studied PGDE and MA in Philosophy in Nnamdi Azikiwe University, Awka. He is currently undertaking post-graduate studies in Igbo Language and related languages in the same University.

Other books by the author:
The ploughman (2000)
Democracy (2001)
Good English Grammar (2002)
Ozuzuoke n' ime Chineke (2003)
The *Igbos* are still in Political University, UNIPOL (2004)
Ndi Amuma Ugha na Ndi Ashawo Uka (2004)
Our Confused Christians (2005)
Uwa Onye na Chi ya (2006)
Ọrụ Ndị Mmụọma N'ebe Anyị Nọ (2007)

www.ingramcontent.com/pod-product-compliance
Lightning Source LLC
Chambersburg PA
CBHW020552030426
42337CB00013B/1068